THE ULTIMATE GEN Z DICTIONARY

Vibhavari Lanjekar

BlueRose ONE.com
Stories Matter
NewDelhi • London

BLUEROSE PUBLISHERS
India | U.K.

BlueRose ONE.com
Stories Matter
NewDelhi • London

For permissions requests or inquiries regarding this publication, please contact:

BLUEROSE PUBLISHERS
www.BlueRoseONE.com
info@bluerosepublishers.com
+91 8882 898 898
+4407342408967

ISBN: 978-93-7310-637-3

Cover design: Yash Singhal
Typesetting: Namrata Saini

First Edition: September 2025

100 Dictionary words

1. No Cap

Meaning: No lie / Seriously
Use in Sentence: "This pizza is the best thing I've ever had, no cap."
Emoji Vibe: 🧢❌
Fun Note: If you *are* lying, people just say "Cap!" — basically calling you out.

2. Slay

Meaning: To do something really well / Look amazing
Use in Sentence: "You slayed that outfit, bestie!"
Emoji Vibe: 💅🔥👑
Fun Note: From fashion culture to everyday wins.

3. It's Giving...

Meaning: It's serving a certain vibe / feels like
Use in Sentence: "It's giving rich aunt energy."
Emoji Vibe: 🎁✨
Fun Note: Add drama. Add flair. Add anything.

4. Bet

Meaning: Okay / Deal / Challenge accepted
Use in Sentence: "You think I won't? Bet."
Emoji Vibe: 🤝🎯
Fun Note: One word, many moods.

5. Mid

Meaning: Average / Not impressive
Use in Sentence: "The movie was mid, nothing special."
Emoji Vibe: 😐□
Fun Note: The worst compliment.

6. Rizz

Meaning: Charm / Flirting game
Use in Sentence: "He's got mad rizz."
Emoji Vibe: 😎💬💘
Fun Note: From TikTok to pop culture.

7. Sus

Meaning: Suspicious / Sketchy
Use in Sentence: "Why's he being so sus about his phone?"
Emoji Vibe: 🕵️👀
Fun Note: Made famous by *Among Us*.

8. Dead

Meaning: That's hilarious / I can't even
Use in Sentence: "You wore that to school?! I'm dead 💀"
Emoji Vibe: 💀😂
Fun Note: Gen Z's way of saying ROFL.

9. Flex

Meaning: Show off
Use in Sentence: "Posting your vacation pics? Nice flex."
Emoji Vibe: 💪😎
Fun Note: Also used sarcastically.

10. Bestie

Meaning: Friend / Friendly nickname (even strangers)
Use in Sentence: "You got this, bestie 💖"
Emoji Vibe: 💖👯🌈
Fun Note: Even when roasting someone.

11. Main Character

Meaning: Someone living their best life / center of attention
Use in Sentence: "Walking down the street like a main character."
Emoji Vibe: 🎬🌟
Fun Note: A compliment for being bold and confident.

12. Ratioed

Meaning: When replies or quotes > likes (usually bad)
Use in Sentence: "He got ratioed so hard on that tweet."
Emoji Vibe: 📉💬
Fun Note: Twitter/X slang — not a good look.

13. Simp

Meaning: Someone who does too much for someone they like
Use in Sentence: "He's simping over that influencer again."
Emoji Vibe: 😍□
Fun Note: Not always negative — can also mean sweet or loyal.

14. Boujee

Meaning: Fancy, luxurious, high-maintenance
Use in Sentence: "That brunch spot is so boujee."
Emoji Vibe: 💅🥂✨
Fun Note: From "bourgeois" — extra with elegance.

15. Cheugy

Meaning: Out of style / trying too hard
Use in Sentence: "Skinny jeans? That's kinda cheugy now."
Emoji Vibe: 😬👖📅
Fun Note: Gen Z's gentle way of saying "not it."

16. Ghosted

Meaning: Suddenly cut off contact with someone
Use in Sentence: "We were texting all week, then she ghosted me."
Emoji Vibe: 👻📵
Fun Note: Haunting but in dating.

17. Lowkey / Highkey

Meaning: Lowkey = secretly, Highkey = very much so
Use in Sentence: "I lowkey love that song." / "I highkey need coffee."
Emoji Vibe: 🔑📶
Fun Note: Sliders for feelings.

18. W

Meaning: Win / Success / Good thing
Use in Sentence: "Got the job? That's a W!"
Emoji Vibe: 🏆✅
Fun Note: "W" = Win. "L" = Loss.

19. Vibe Check

Meaning: Assessing the energy/mood of someone or something
Use in Sentence: "This party failed the vibe check."
Emoji Vibe: ✨🧠🎧
Fun Note: A spiritual energy test.

20. Clap Back

Meaning: A sharp, clever response to criticism
Use in Sentence: "She clapped back hard at the trolls."
Emoji Vibe: 👏🔥💬
Fun Note: Mic drop moment.

21. Cringe

Meaning: Embarrassing or awkward behavior
Use in Sentence: "That TikTok dance is so cringe."
Emoji Vibe: 😬🙈
Fun Note: The ultimate Gen Z diss. Cringe = not cool.

22. Salty

Meaning: Bitter or upset over something minor
Use in Sentence: "He's still salty about losing the game."
Emoji Vibe: 🧂😤
Fun Note: A tasty way to express pettiness.

23. Glow Up

Meaning: An impressive transformation (looks, style, confidence)
Use in Sentence: "She had a serious glow up since high school."
Emoji Vibe: ✨📈💄
Fun Note: From awkward to awesome.

24. Stan

Meaning: To obsessively support someone or something
Use in Sentence: "I stan that singer so hard."
Emoji Vibe: 🙌🎤💯
Fun Note: Inspired by Eminem's song "Stan" — now a badge of fandom.

25. Snack

Meaning: Someone who looks really good
Use in Sentence: "Wow, he's a whole snack."
Emoji Vibe: 🍫👀🔥
Fun Note: Can upgrade to "full meal" if extremely attractive.

26. Go Off

Meaning: Express yourself freely / Keep doing your thing
Use in Sentence: "You roasted him? Go off, queen!"
Emoji Vibe: 🔥💁‍♀️👏
Fun Note: Hype mode: activated.

27. Mood

Meaning: Relatable emotion or vibe
Use in Sentence: *[posts pic of cat sleeping]* — "Mood."
Emoji Vibe: 😴😩💯
Fun Note: The universal reaction.

28. Periodt

Meaning: Emphasizing the finality of a statement
Use in Sentence: "I'm done arguing. Periodt."
Emoji Vibe: 🛑💅🔚
Fun Note: Add a "t" for drama. Used to shut down debates.

29. Yeet

Meaning: To throw something with force / Exclamation of excitement
Use in Sentence: "She just yeeted her phone across the room!"
Emoji Vibe: 🌀📱💨
Fun Note: Means *throw* or *yay* depending on context.

30. L

Meaning: Loss / Failure / Bad move
Use in Sentence: "He took an L on that test."
Emoji Vibe: ❌📉😓
Fun Note: Short and brutal. The opposite of a "W."

31. Hits Different

Meaning: Feels unique or more intense than usual
Use in Sentence: "That song just hits different at 2 a.m."
Emoji Vibe: 🎧💔🌙
Fun Note: For when the vibes are *next level.*

32. Vibe

Meaning: Atmosphere, energy, or feeling of something
Use in Sentence: "This cafe has such a chill vibe."
Emoji Vibe: □☕🌿
Fun Note: Used for everything—from outfits to people.

33. Ate

Meaning: Did amazing / Nailed it
Use in Sentence: "She ate that performance!"
Emoji Vibe: 🍽🔥👏
Fun Note: Often followed by "and left no crumbs."

34. Ick

Meaning: Sudden turn-off or cringe moment
Use in Sentence: "He clapped when the plane landed—major ick."
Emoji Vibe: 🚩😬🧊
Fun Note: Once you feel it, there's no going back.

35. Bussin

Meaning: Really good, especially food
Use in Sentence: "This pasta is bussin fr."
Emoji Vibe: 🍝😋🔥
Fun Note: Usually said twice for emphasis—"bussin bussin."

36. Skrrt

Meaning: Sound of tires / To leave quickly
Use in Sentence: "As soon as I saw him coming, I skrrt out."
Emoji Vibe: 🚗💨😳
Fun Note: From rap lyrics to awkward exits.

37. Big Yikes

Meaning: Major embarrassment or awkwardness
Use in Sentence: "He texted his ex by mistake. Big yikes."
Emoji Vibe: 😳🚫🙃
Fun Note: Yikes — but amplified.

38. Screaming

Meaning: Overwhelmed by emotion (funny, shocking, etc.)
Use in Sentence: *[sees dramatic meme]* — "I'm screaming 😂"
Emoji Vibe: 😭💀📢
Fun Note: No actual screaming required.

39. Pushin P

Meaning: Keeping it real / Maintaining positivity
Use in Sentence: "Helping your friend? That's pushin P."
Emoji Vibe: 🅿️💛💯
Fun Note: P = player, peace, positivity (origin: Gunna song).

40. Zaddy

Meaning: Attractive, stylish, confident man
Use in Sentence: "Look at him in that suit — total zaddy."
Emoji Vibe: 🕶️💼🔥
Fun Note: Think dad vibes, but fashionable.

41. Viral

Meaning: Widely shared on the internet
Use in Sentence: "Her video went viral overnight."
Emoji Vibe: 📲🚀📈
Fun Note: Instant fame. Sometimes accidental.

42. Boujee

Meaning: Fancy or high-class in a flashy way
Use in Sentence: "That restaurant is way too boujee for me."
Emoji Vibe: 👜🥂💎
Fun Note: Living the glam life (even if it's fake).

43. Drip

Meaning: Cool style, especially clothes or accessories
Use in Sentence: "Check out his drip — that jacket is fire."
Emoji Vibe: 💧👟🔥
Fun Note: The more drip, the more style points.

44. On God

Meaning: For real / I swear
Use in Sentence: "That was the best burger ever, on God."
Emoji Vibe: ✝🙌😤
Fun Note: Used for strong emphasis and truth.

45. Shook

Meaning: Surprised or shocked
Use in Sentence: "He showed up at my house—I was shook."
Emoji Vibe: 😲🙀⚡
Fun Note: One word for being emotionally rattled.

46. Savage

Meaning: Bold, ruthless, or brutally honest
Use in Sentence: "She told him off in front of everyone—savage!"
Emoji Vibe: 🐯🔥🗣️
Fun Note: Often used as a compliment.

47. Drag

Meaning: To criticize or roast someone harshly
Use in Sentence: "She dragged him for that weak apology."
Emoji Vibe: 🧹🗯️💣
Fun Note: Often hilarious. Sometimes brutal.

48. Say Less

Meaning: Got it / Understood / No need to explain
Use in Sentence: "You need help moving? Say less."
Emoji Vibe: 🤐👍🚚
Fun Note: A cooler way to agree.

49. Tapped In

Meaning: Aware, connected, focused
Use in Sentence: "She's really tapped in to the fashion world."
Emoji Vibe: 📡💡🧠
Fun Note: Like being in the loop—just smarter.

50. Let Them Cook

Meaning: Let someone do their thing without interference
Use in Sentence: *[friend explaining a wild idea]* — "Shh, let them cook."
Emoji Vibe: 🍳🤔🔥
Fun Note: Sometimes genius starts weird.

51. I'm Weak

Meaning: Something is extremely funny
Use in Sentence: "That meme? I'm weak 😂"
Emoji Vibe: 🤣💀🙈
Vibe Check: Used when you're laughing too hard to even respond properly.

52. Cap

Meaning: A lie or exaggeration
Use in Sentence: "You met Rihanna? That's cap."
Emoji Vibe: 🧢🙄✋
Vibe Check: Accuse gently—or don't. It's all about tone.

53. Touch Grass

Meaning: Go outside / Take a break from online life
Use in Sentence: "You've been arguing online for 4 hours—go touch grass."
Emoji Vibe: 🌱📴🌤️
Vibe Check: Digital detox, Gen Z style.

54. Based

Meaning: Unapologetically true or authentic
Use in Sentence: "You said what we're all thinking. Based."
Emoji Vibe: 🧠💥📢
Vibe Check: Compliment for brave honesty.

55. Canon Event

Meaning: A moment that shapes your personal storyline
Use in Sentence: "Getting ghosted? Yeah, that was my canon event."
Emoji Vibe: 🎥📖😩
Vibe Check: Let it happen. No one can interfere.

56. Gatekeep

Meaning: To withhold information to maintain exclusivity
Use in Sentence: "Don't gatekeep that skincare routine."
Emoji Vibe: 🚪🔐💅
Vibe Check: Gen Z believes in sharing the hacks (usually).

57. Delulu

Meaning: Being delusional (in a funny or dreamy way)
Use in Sentence: "He liked my post. I'm delulu, but we're basically dating."
Emoji Vibe: 🤪💭❤️
Vibe Check: Main character fantasy energy.

58. NPC

Meaning: Someone who seems basic or robotic
Use in Sentence: "He just walked in, said 'Hi,' and walked out. Total NPC."
Emoji Vibe: 🕹️🤖🚶
Vibe Check: Low effort social presence.

59. Slaps

Meaning: Really good (especially music)
Use in Sentence: "This song slaps hard."
Emoji Vibe: 🎶🙌🔥
Vibe Check: When it hits your soul just right.

60. Core

Meaning: A defining aesthetic or vibe
Use in Sentence: "That's so cottagecore."
Emoji Vibe: 🌸📷🧺
Vibe Check: If it ends in "-core," it's a whole lifestyle.

💘 RELATIONSHIP & DATING SLANG (61–80)

61. Simp

Meaning: Someone who does *too much* for someone they like
Use in Sentence: "He brought her coffee *again*? What a simp."
Emoji Vibe: 😍□☕
Vibe Check: Love-struck and proud (but might get roasted).

62. Rizz

Meaning: Charm or flirting game
Use in Sentence: "He's got no rizz. Just vibes and silence."
Emoji Vibe: 😏🧃💬
Vibe Check: Can you pull? Then you got the rizz.

63. Thirst Trap

Meaning: A hot post meant to get attention
Use in Sentence: "New gym pic? Obvious thirst trap."
Emoji Vibe: 🔥📷💦
Vibe Check: You know your angles. Respect.

64. Cuffing Season

Meaning: Time of year (usually winter) when people look for serious relationships
Use in Sentence: "It's getting cold. Must be cuffing season."
Emoji Vibe: ❄💑☕
Vibe Check: From single to snuggled in 0.2 seconds.

65. Hard Launch

Meaning: Publicly revealing your relationship online
Use in Sentence: "She posted a couple pic—total hard launch."
Emoji Vibe: 📷💍🌐
Vibe Check: No more soft hints. Full reveal.

66. Soft Launch

Meaning: Subtle hints you're dating someone (like a hand or shadow in a photo)
Use in Sentence: "That mirror pic? Total soft launch vibes."
Emoji Vibe: □✋💋
Vibe Check: Mysterious but make it romantic.

67. Caught Feelings

Meaning: Started developing romantic emotions
Use in Sentence: "I thought it was casual... but I caught feelings."
Emoji Vibe: 💘😩🤷‍♀️
Vibe Check: Uh-oh. It's real now.

68. Benched

Meaning: Kept as a romantic backup
Use in Sentence: "She texts me only when she's bored—I'm benched."
Emoji Vibe: 🪑📵😶
Vibe Check: Not first pick, but still in the game.

69. Situationship

Meaning: More than a fling, less than a relationship
Use in Sentence: "We hang out a lot, but it's not official—it's a situationship."
Emoji Vibe: 💛😬📉
Vibe Check: Feelings + confusion = this.

70. Ghosted

Meaning: Cut off all communication without explanation
Use in Sentence: "One day we were talking nonstop… then nothing. I got ghosted."
Emoji Vibe: 👻📵💔
Vibe Check: Brutal. Cold. Classic Gen Z move.

71. Kittenfishing

Meaning: Slightly exaggerating who you are online (but not full catfish)
Use in Sentence: "He said he's 6ft but showed up 5'7—kittenfishing alert!"
Emoji Vibe: 🐱📏📱
Vibe Check: Not a total lie, but not the truth either.

72. Pocketing

Meaning: Hiding someone you're dating from your friends or family
Use in Sentence: "We've been dating for months, but I haven't met anyone. I think I'm being pocketed."
Emoji Vibe: 👖🤐🙄
Vibe Check: If you're hidden, it's shady.

73. Orbiting

Meaning: They ghosted you but still watch your stories and like your posts
Use in Sentence: "He hasn't texted in weeks, but views everything. He's orbiting me!"
Emoji Vibe: 🛰️👀📲
Vibe Check: Ghost, but make it clingy.

74. Haunting

Meaning: When an ex pops back with random likes or DMs
Use in Sentence: "He liked my 2019 post. Is he haunting me??"
Emoji Vibe: 👻🕸️💬
Vibe Check: They're not back… they're just being weird.

75. Textationship

Meaning: A relationship that exists mostly or only through texting
Use in Sentence: "We've never met, but we text 24/7. It's a total textationship."
Emoji Vibe: 📱💭□
Vibe Check: Real feelings, virtual world.

76. Cushioning

Meaning: Flirting with others while in a relationship to soften a potential breakup
Use in Sentence: "She's got backup plans already? That's cushioning."
Emoji Vibe: 🛋️😶💔
Vibe Check: If you're the cushion, you're not the priority.

77. Insta-official

Meaning: Making a relationship official via Instagram
Use in Sentence: "They went Insta-official with that beach pic!"
Emoji Vibe: 📷🌊💑
Vibe Check: If it's not on the feed, is it even real?

78. Zombie-ing

Meaning: When someone who ghosted you suddenly comes back from the dead

Use in Sentence: "After months of silence, he just messaged 'hey'—zombie-ing hard."

Emoji Vibe: 🧟📩□

Vibe Check: Back from the dead... and still trash.

79. Sneaky Link

Meaning: A secret hookup or relationship

Use in Sentence: "No one knows about us. You're my sneaky link."

Emoji Vibe: 🤫🔗😈

Vibe Check: Private. Spicy. Under the radar.

80. Love Triangle

Meaning: When three people are romantically tangled

Use in Sentence: "He's into her, she's into me, and I'm confused—total love triangle."

Emoji Vibe: 🔺💘😵💫

Vibe Check: Messy drama, main character plot.

📲 SOCIAL MEDIA SLANG (71–90)

81. Sus

Meaning: Suspicious, sketchy, or shady behavior
Use in Sentence: "He said he was home but I saw him on Snap maps downtown. Kinda sus."
Emoji Vibe: 🧐🚩👀
Vibe Check: Red flag alert. Trust issues activated.

82. Ick

Meaning: A sudden turn-off or something that kills attraction
Use in Sentence: "He clapped when the plane landed. Immediate ick."
Emoji Vibe: 😬🧼🙅‍♀️
Vibe Check: Cringe. Can't unsee it. Bye forever.

83. Ratioed

Meaning: When replies or comments outnumber likes — usually a sign of disapproval
Use in Sentence: "She tried to cancel him but got ratioed into oblivion."
Emoji Vibe: 🔢📉📱
Vibe Check: Public L. The internet has spoken.

84. Main Character

Meaning: Someone owning the moment, like the star of their own movie
Use in Sentence: "She walked into the room like the main character."
Emoji Vibe: 🎬💁‍♀️🌟
Vibe Check: Confident. Cinematic. All eyes on you.

85. Bussin

Meaning: Extremely good, especially food
Use in Sentence: "This ramen is actually bussin fr."
Emoji Vibe: 🍜😋🔥
Vibe Check: Delicious. 10/10. Tastebud party.

86. POV

Meaning: Point of view, often used to describe a situation through someone's lens
Use in Sentence: "POV: You're stuck in a group project with slackers."
Emoji Vibe: 🎥👁️🧠
Vibe Check: Relatable. Meme-ready. First-person feels.

87. Valid

Meaning: Genuine, respectable, impressive
Use in Sentence: "That take was valid. I respect it."
Emoji Vibe: ✅🤝🧠
Vibe Check: Certified. Co-signed. Green check energy.

88. Gyatt

Meaning: Slang for noticing someone with a curvy body, often exaggerated
Use in Sentence: "GYATT! She walked by and broke necks fr."
Emoji Vibe: 👀🍑💥
Vibe Check: Thirsty. Loud. Horny on main.

89. Slay

Meaning: To do something incredibly well or look amazing
Use in Sentence: "You slayed that presentation. Like, wow."
Emoji Vibe: 👑💃✨
Vibe Check: Powerful. Fierce. Queen behavior.

90. L

Meaning: Loss, failure, or embarrassing moment
Use in Sentence: "Missed the bus and spilled coffee? That's a fat L."
Emoji Vibe: 🅰⬇💀
Vibe Check: Tough. Laugh it off. Tomorrow's a new day.

81. Main Character

Meaning: Feeling like your life is a movie and you're the star
Use in Sentence: "Walking through the rain with my playlist—main character vibes."
Emoji Vibe: 🎬🎧🌧
Vibe Check: Self-love and cinematic drama.

82. Algos

Meaning: Short for "algorithms," the tech that decides what you see
Use in Sentence: "The algos knew I needed that cat video today."
Emoji Vibe: 📊🤖📲
Vibe Check: The invisible hand of social media.

83. Shadow Banned

Meaning: When your posts don't show up due to app limits, without notice
Use in Sentence: "I swear I'm shadow banned. No one's seeing my posts!"
Emoji Vibe: 🚫👻📉
Vibe Check: Social media ghost mode.

84. Simp

Meaning: Someone who does too much for someone they like
Use in Sentence: "He drove 3 hours to bring her coffee. Simp energy."
Emoji Vibe: 💘🚗🥺
Vibe Check: Hopelessly devoted or just too much?

85. Vibe Check

Meaning: Testing the mood or energy of someone/something
Use in Sentence: "She entered the room and failed the vibe check."
Emoji Vibe: 🌡️🧘😬
Vibe Check: Mood validation required.

86. Alt

Meaning: Alternative version of your main account or persona
Use in Sentence: "That's my alt—don't tell anyone."
Emoji Vibe: 👤🔒😎
Vibe Check: Private thoughts, low-key vibes.

87. Going Live

Meaning: Broadcasting yourself in real-time on social platforms
Use in Sentence: "Going live in 10! Come hang."
Emoji Vibe: 🎥📡💬
Vibe Check: Real-time attention.

88. TikTok Brain

Meaning: Short attention span caused by fast content
Use in Sentence: "I can't focus anymore. I've got TikTok brain."
Emoji Vibe: 🧠📱⚡
Vibe Check: Gen Z's digital side effect.

89. Repost Rage

Meaning: The annoyance when someone reposts your meme without credit

Use in Sentence: "Ugh, he stole my meme. Repost rage is real."

Emoji Vibe: 😤🔁📷

Vibe Check: Tag or drag.

90. Social Battery

Meaning: Your mental energy for being around people or online

Use in Sentence: "Can't go out—my social battery's dead."

Emoji Vibe: 🔋😮💨🛏️

Vibe Check: Energy-saving mode.

🌈 GEN Z VIBE CHECK WRAP-UP (91–100)

91. It's Giving

Meaning: Used to describe the energy/vibe of something

Use in Sentence: "That outfit? It's giving ICON."

Emoji Vibe: 💅👑✨

Vibe Check: Big style energy.

92. Skrrt

Meaning: Sound of speeding away / dramatic exit

Use in Sentence: "This convo is awkward—skrrt!"

Emoji Vibe: 🏎️💨✌️

Vibe Check: Exit, stage left.

93. Big Yikes

Meaning: Extra embarrassing or cringe

Use in Sentence: "He proposed over text? Big yikes."

Emoji Vibe: 😬📵🙈

Vibe Check: Secondhand embarrassment.

94. Screaming, Crying, Throwing Up

Meaning: Extreme emotional reaction (good or bad)
Use in Sentence: "She liked my post. I'm screaming, crying, throwing up."
Emoji Vibe: 😭🤯🤢
Vibe Check: Overwhelmed.com.

95. Say Less

Meaning: I got it / Understood quickly
Use in Sentence: "You want pizza? Say less."
Emoji Vibe: 🤫👌📦
Vibe Check: Instant agreement.

96. Sus

Meaning: Suspicious / Shady
Use in Sentence: "That excuse was sus."
Emoji Vibe: 🕵️😕🚩
Vibe Check: 🚨 Trust issues activated.

97. Glow-Up

Meaning: A major positive transformation
Use in Sentence: "Her glow-up over summer break? Unreal."
Emoji Vibe: ✨📷🔥
Vibe Check: Self-improvement flex.

98. Deadass

Meaning: Totally serious / For real
Use in Sentence: "Deadass, I'm not joking."
Emoji Vibe: 😐✔🧃
Vibe Check: No cap, all facts.

99. No Thoughts, Just Vibes

Meaning: Going with the flow, chill mindset
Use in Sentence: "Me at the beach: no thoughts, just vibes."
Emoji Vibe: 🌊😌□
Vibe Check: Brain off, peace on.

100. Period

Meaning: Used to emphasize a point; end of discussion
Use in Sentence: "She's the best to ever do it. Periodt."
Emoji Vibe: 👏🛑💯
Vibe Check: Final word energy.

🎮 GEN Z GAME TIME – *"Slang Showdown!"*

🔤 Match the Slang!

Match the Gen Z term to its correct meaning:

A Slang Term	B Meaning
1 Ghosted	a Being totally ignored
2 Delulu	b Attention-seeking post
3 Main Character	c You're the star of your own life
4 Rizz	d Charm or flirting skill
5 Thirst Trap	e Funny, dreamy delusion

Answer Key: 1–a, 2–e, 3–c, 4–d, 5–b ✅

✍️ Finish the Sentence

Fill in the blanks using Gen Z terms:

1. When something's super funny, I say "I'm ______."
2. That outfit? It's giving ______.
3. She left me on read for 3 days. I've been totally ______.
4. That remix ______! I've been replaying it all day.
5. My social ______ is low—I need alone time.

🧩 Decode the Emojis

Can you guess the slang word from the emojis?

1. 🤪💭❤️ = ________
2. 🧢🙄✋ = ________
3. 🔋😮💨🛏️ = ________
4. 👏🛑💯 = ________
5. 🕹️🤖🚶 = ________

Delulu or Realulu?

He liked 2 of your posts in a row

Delulu ☐ Realulu

He suddenly texted you 'hey'

Delulu ☐ Realulu

He planned an actual date

Delulu ☐ Realulu

She posted your hand on her story

Delulu ☐ Realulu

SLANG SELFIE CHALLENGE

Snap & share your best slang-inspired selfies!

RIZZ 😉

DELULU 😨

GHOSTED 😟

SOFT LAUNCH

CERTIFIED
GEN Z

SLAY
QUEEN

RIZZ
MASTER

VIBE
CHECKED!

Vibe

Vibha

TOUCH
GRASS
CREW

DELULU
BUT CUTE

NO CAP
ZONE

SLAY
ERA

IT'S
GIVING

MENTALLY
I'M HERE

STAN
STAN
MODE

STAN
ICK

REALITY CHECK
MOOD
NGL
OUT OF POCKET

CERTIFIED GEN Z

THIS CERTIFIES THAT

YOUR NAME

HAS SUCCESSFULLY COMPLETED THIS VIBE CHECK

DATE

💔 Soft Launched & Ghosted

🧃 _A love story with filters, followers, and fallout._

📱 **Main Characters:**

- **Zoya** (17): Artsy, funny, posts poetry and playlists.
- **Rehaan** (18): Campus crush, meme king, private account energy.
- **Arya** (Zoya's BFF): Human lie detector, walks with ✨main character✨ energy.

📖 **Story:**

Zoya was not delulu.
Okay, maybe a little. But *Rehaan started it.*

It began with him replying to her story:
🖼️ *"This vibe >>>>"*
Then a follow.
Then daily reactions.
Then 3 a.m. convos that turned into "wyd?" at 2 p.m.

She didn't tell anyone.
Only Arya knew.
Because it wasn't *official-official.*
It was a **soft launch situationship.**

One day, he posted a pic:

🎮 Controller in hand, captioned "Player 2 needed."

Zoya replied:

"I call dibs 💅 "

He liked it.
Then heart-reacted to her selfie.
Then said, *"You look like the type who breaks hearts and paints sunsets."*
Zoya melted like a Ring Pop in summer.

But then…
He stopped replying.
Left her on read.

Posted new stories with some girl tagged as "🤍✨"

Zoya zoomed in.
The bracelet on that girl's hand?
The one Zoya gifted him during their "let's-not-label-this" phase?

Betrayal.
In HD.

Zoya didn't cry.
Okay, she did. For 10 minutes. Then put on gloss.

The next day, she posted a full-body fit check with the caption:
"She upgraded. New chapter unlocked."

Rehaan viewed it in 3 seconds.
Didn't like it.
Didn't comment.

But he saw it.
And that was enough.

Arya sent a voice note:
"Babe, you just ate. No crumbs."

Zoya replied,
"I'm done being 'Player 2'. I *am* the game."

✨ **Moral (Gen Z Style):**

💗 *Soft launch if you want. But never forget — you're the full drop.*

🎧 *Delulu can be solulu… but never forget to glow up harder than you break down.*

📴 *When they ghost, you post.*

Soft Launched & Ghosted

A love story with filters, followers, and fallout

💔 Left on Delivered, Still in Love

📱 **Plot**:
A guy named Kabeer replies to all of Rhea's memes, sends her Spotify playlists titled "for u <3", and says "we're soul-linked."
But suddenly... his replies turn into just "delivered."
But not blocked. Not unfollowed. Just slowly... fading.
Rhea has to decide: confront him? Or mute and move on?

👀 **Twist**: He had a gf the whole time — and Rhea finds out through a tagged birthday story.

😍Main Character Moodboard

🎬**Plot**:
Tia has always felt like the sidekick. Quiet. Background energy.
But after a haircut, deleting an ex's playlist, and uploading a "main character photo dump," she starts getting DMs — especially from her old crush who now says: "lowkey had a thing for you always."
But this time… SHE leaves *him* on read.

👑 **Ending line**:
"I wasn't invisible. They just had bad taste."

Tia had always felt like the sidekick.
Quiet. Background energy.

I wasn't invisible. They just had bad taste.

Delulu But Hopeful

Jay's been in love with his best friend Mira for… ever, maybe.
She sends him TikToks captioned *"this is so us lol,"*
hugs him like the world's about to end,
texts *"miss you"* at 1:43 a.m.—
the kind of moments that feel scripted.
Rom-com coded.
He starts to think: maybe this isn't just friendship.
Maybe it's *them.*

One night, heart pounding louder than the bass in her car,
he tells her.
"I think I like you. Like, more than a friend."

She laughs, light and confused.
"Wait… like, seriously?"

And in that second,
he sees the full movie reel rewind—
the hugs, the texts, the shared playlists—
all playing in a genre he was watching alone.

He walks home alone that night.
Same playlist in his headphones.
But when her song comes on,
he skips it.
Finally.

💅 Soft Blocked, Hard Feelings

🚫**Plot**:
Rumi thought she was over her ex until she accidentally liked his new girl's photo from her finsta.
Next thing she knows — she's soft-blocked.
Not unfollowed. But gone. Quietly.
So she hosts a "Block Party" — a night with her friends to block everyone who brings bad energy.

💥 **Ending line**:
"Some people aren't meant to be muted. They're meant to be deleted."

Page 1 – Notification Silence

Lia Kapoor's phone buzzed. Again.
But this time, she didn't look. She was two weeks into her digital detox — not because of some mindfulness trend — but because she had no choice. Her account got hacked after she downloaded a shady-looking AI-filter app called "GlowFi."

Snap gone. Insta gone. Her phone, basically a calculator now.

She walked through her college canteen, unnoticed. No one whispered "OMG Lia posted fire last night." No one double-tapped her coffee. She didn't post one.

And surprisingly… she didn't hate it.

Her old notebook — not the Notes app, a real spiral one — now held doodles, random lyrics, even actual feelings. That day, she wrote:

"Feels like I unplugged from the Matrix. Do I even exist without a story?"

That's when she saw it. A sticker on a bench:
"Are you more than your WiFi?"

It had a tiny QR code, ironic, considering her situation. But curiosity always wins.

Page 2 – The Secret Society of the Unseen

Next day, she scanned the code using her friend Vihaan's phone.

It opened a low-res webpage. Basic. Retro vibes. One sentence:

"Meet us. 6:30 PM. Library basement. Come with no devices."

Creepy? A little. But Lia had nothing left to lose. She missed being curious more than being popular.

At 6:28 PM, she was at the college library. No phone. No AirPods. Just a pen, a notebook, and slight nervousness.

She walked into the old basement where ancient books gathered dust. There, in dim fairy lights, sat five people. Different, awkward, a little off-grid. But all smiling.

They called themselves **"The Offline."**

"We're not anti-tech," said Arjun, the oldest. "We're just pro-real. Once a week, we share stories without screens."

No judging. No filters. Just feelings. Lia sat. Then she spoke. Really spoke. And everyone listened like she mattered — not her selfie, not her followers. **Her.**

Page 3 – Rebooted But Woke

Weeks passed. Lia's socials were back, finally.

But something had shifted.

She didn't post everything anymore. She didn't scroll till her neck hurt. She started replying late. But meaningfully.

Her stories were now real — small things. A note to a stranger. Her cat's stupid sneeze. Her fear of not being enough. And slowly, people noticed that this new Lia… felt more *alive.*

One day, someone DMed her:

"I read your story about being offline. I thought I was the only one. Thanks."

And Lia smiled. Not because she got likes.
Because she got through.

The "Offline" crew still met every Thursday.
No tags. No likes. Just life.

"Can We Not?" – A Gen Z Office Tale

Characters:

Raya (23): UX designer, proud bisexual, wears chunky rings and Crocs to work.

Arman (28): Gen Z-coded millennial, team lead who "gets it".

Debashree Ma'am (52): HR, says "zooming" for every online call.

📂 Scene 1: The Email That Started It All

Raya sits at her desk, sipping overpriced cold brew, when an email lands.

Subject: *"Office Dress Code Reminder – No Casual Footwear, Ripped Jeans, or Overly Vibrant Hair."*

Raya stares at her lavender hair reflected in her screen. *Overly vibrant?*
Her Slack pings:
Arman: "You saw it too? Are we in a '90s bank now?"

📂 Scene 2: #SilentRebellion

The next day, Raya walks in wearing neon green Crocs, socks that say *"Unbothered"*, and hair clips spelling "NO."
The designer team follows. One has glitter on their cheeks. Another has a tote that says *"We Are Not Our KPIs."*

At 3:00 PM, HR walks by. She blinks.
"You all look... colorful."

Raya replies calmly, "Oh, we're just aligning with our inner selves."

📂 Scene 3: The Unplanned Presentation

A client shows up early. Everyone panics—except the Gen Z team.

Raya plugs in her MacBook, opens Canva, and runs a bold, meme-laced, perfectly timed pitch that ends with:
"Users don't want to feel managed. They want to feel seen."

Silence. Then applause.
Debashree Ma'am claps too. "Okay... this was very... zooming."

📂 **Scene 4: "What Even *Is* Professionalism?"**

Later that week, HR calls for a "feedback circle" (which they renamed from *meeting* after complaints).

They sit in a circle of bean bags. Raya says:
"Professionalism should include identity, not erase it. My Crocs didn't ruin the pitch. Your outdated email almost did."

Arman backs her. "Let's evolve, not enforce."

📂 **Final Scene: New Dress Code (Beta)**

A month later, a poster is pinned in the office café:

💼 **New Dress Code Policy – 2.0 (Pilot)**

✔️ Express Yourself

✔️ Respect Others

✗ No judgment

✨ Crocs welcome

At the bottom: "Created with Raya & team."

CAN WE NOT?

A Gen Z office scene